JODI BOYER

Emmie

and the

Accidental

Unicorn

ILLUSTRATIONS BY
RUSTY BOYER

ISBN-13: 978-1-7360734-0-7
ISBN: 1-7360734-0-0

With love,
Aunt Jodi & Uncle Rusty

CONTENTS

1

Introducing
~~Emmie~~ Hannah

Don't let the title fool you. This story is not about Emmie Button. It isn't a story about a precocious eight-year-old with long, light brown hair and big brown eyes who loved to dance, swim, and read. This story won't take you on a journey through Emmie's messy bedroom, with all of its cozy, colorful pillows, stuffed animals, and arts and crafts strewn about the floor. It won't be about her hip-hop recitals or her new love for roller skating. You won't read about Emmie's favorite family vacations, or about her adventures in elementary school. Nope, this story is not about Emmie Button. This story is about Emmie's big sister, Hannah.

Emmie loved playing with her big sister. When they were little, they would play all of the time! Emmie's favorite memory was dressing like princesses and singing along to their favorite movies. She also remembered chasing bubbles in the backyard, as Hannah blew them from the patio. Now that Hannah was a preteen, she didn't want to play pretend or blow bubbles. Hannah was taller and stronger than Emmie, which made it easy for Hannah to push Emmie out of her bedroom when she didn't want to play, which was often. To Emmie, it seemed like Hannah only wanted to hang out with her friends or text on her phone.

The worst part was that Emmie was always getting into trouble. Whenever Hannah had friends over, Emmie was left out, and her parents always took Hannah's side. She'd ask nicely to play with Hannah, and Hannah would tell her that she was too little and couldn't play with the big kids. From what Emmie could tell, they weren't even having fun. The preteens didn't play at all. They just stared at their phones. Emmie would walk into Hannah's room with her tablet, ready to join the group, but Hannah would push her out of the room and lock the door behind her. At that point, Mom or Dad would get mad at Emmie and tell her to go to her room. They never yelled at Hannah. Hannah was clearly the favorite child.

What Emmie didn't know is that Hannah felt the same way. Well, sort of. To Hannah, it was clear that Emmie was their parents' favorite daughter. They never yelled at Emmie. Whenever Hannah had friends over, her parents would tell her to be kind to her little sister and to let her play with them. They always took Emmie's side.

The worst part about it was that Emmie was always getting into trouble, and Hannah always got blamed for it. Mom and Dad would tell Hannah that she was the oldest and that she knew better. They had higher expectations of Hannah and said that she needed to set a good example for Emmie. Sometimes Hannah didn't want to play with Emmie because it always ended with Hannah getting punished for something she didn't do.

Emmie also didn't understand that Hannah was getting older, and with age came new responsibilities and challenges. Hannah had a good group of friends, but as she got older, it became harder to maintain friendships. And school was getting harder, too! As Hannah went up in grade level, the tests were more challenging and the homework was more time consuming. This required more of Hannah's focus, so when Emmie wanted to play on a school night, Hannah didn't always have the time to join her.

What Emmie didn't know is that sometimes Hannah wished she was still Emmie's age, so she could be more carefree. She envied that Emmie didn't have challenging homework, afterschool activities, and silly fights with friends. What Hannah didn't know is that Emmie was dealing with her own struggles and growth.

Hannah didn't always remember what it was like being eight. She didn't remember how it felt to be the littlest in the household. It felt like the youngest child wasn't taken seriously, even though Emmie was growing and getting older and smarter.

Emmie thought if only she were older, maybe Hannah would still play with her. Maybe they would be best friends. It didn't matter. On each birthday, Emmie got one step closer to Hannah's age, then in a few months, Hannah's birthday came, pushing them apart again. It seemed like an eternity before Emmie would be a preteen, too, and by that time, Hannah would be deep within her teenage years.

While Hannah did whatever she did in her bedroom, Emmie read books. She'd lose track of time. She'd sit down with a book at lunch, and the next thing she knew, Dad was calling her downstairs for dinner!

Emmie had a reading method. She would tidy her bedroom, then she would arrange her pillows in a specific way that allowed her to be comfortably propped on the bed while resting the book on her knees. She'd have a glass of water on her side table, and she'd snuggle her favorite stuffed dinosaur in her left arm, keeping her right hand free to turn the page.

At the moment, Emmie loved to read about unicorns more than anything. She had several books about them. She often daydreamed about what life would be like if unicorns existed. She thought about riding them through a valley, where the rainbows were made of colorful sprinkles and the clouds were made of marshmallows. Through reading the books *From Moon Drops to Star Shadows: A History of Unicorns* and *Unicorns: A Secret World*, she had become an aficionado of the mythical horned horse.

One day, Mom bought Emmie a new unicorn book, *Your Unicorn Reflection*. She couldn't wait to read it, so she opened it right there on the kitchen table. Within the first few chapters, there was a quiz about the reader's unicorn personality. The quiz was on an elaborately decorated page and included three questions. Emmie traced her index finger over the green vines that led her through the quiz until she landed on her answer. Emmie's Unicorn Reflection was a Sunshine Rider. She flipped the page to discover the descriptions of each possible unicorn. The Sunshine Rider was on the adjacent page under the family of unicorns called Stunning Skylarks. Named for their unique singing abilities, Stunning Skylarks were known for their loving hearts, warmth, and healing song. Emmie traced the words to find Sunshine Rider.

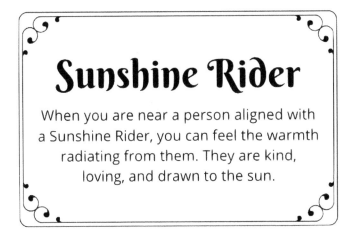

Sunshine Rider

When you are near a person aligned with a Sunshine Rider, you can feel the warmth radiating from them. They are kind, loving, and drawn to the sun.

Emmie gasped. That sounded just like her! She wondered whether the quiz would work for the other members of her family. So she gave Mom the quiz and discovered that her Mom was also a member of the Stunning Skylarks! Mom was a Snow Cloud.

Snow Cloud

As unique as a snowflake, a Snow Cloud's creativity is their own. They are artists, dreamers, and compassionate caregivers.

That described Mom, alright! Mom was pleased with her Unicorn Reflection, too. She set two berry smoothies down on the kitchen island. Emmie grabbed hers and sipped it through the straw.

Hannah walked into the kitchen and, without looking up from her phone, picked up her smoothie.

"Hannah, do you want to know what your Unicorn Reflection is?" Emmie asked.

"Not really," Hannah said.

She picked up the magenta drink and lifted

the straw to her lips.

"Well, can I give you this quiz? It's really fast!" Emmie said.

"Nope," said Hannah.

She started to walk away, but Mom called her back. Mom split Hannah's name into two syllables and held out the second syllable: *Han-naaaah*. This meant Hannah was on the verge of getting in trouble.

Emmie knew this well. When Mom was mad at her, she used Emmie's middle name and also held out the syllable of the middle name: Emmie Jooooo.

Hannah stopped but didn't turn around.

"You have time to take this quick quiz, don't you." Mom didn't ask. She told.

Hannah shrugged, realizing she wasn't going to get out of this one. She would let her sister give her the stupid quiz so she could get back upstairs. Hannah leaned against the kitchen island, slowly sipping her smoothie. The cold quartz countertop hit against her belly at the same time a rush of crushed ice hit her tongue, leading to a brain freeze. She could barely hear her sister's first question.

"I said," Emmie repeated, "Would you rather camp under the stars, make sandcastles on the beach, or ice skate in a secret, snowy forest?"

"Sandcastles, I guess?" Hannah said.

"I said that, too!" Emmie said.

Emmie traced the green vine to the next question.

"If a fairy offered you a choice of gem—"

"Wait—what?" Hannah chortled.

Emmie gave a look of annoyance but repeated herself.

"If a fairy offered you a choice of gem, which would you choose? A ruby (that's a red one), a sapphire (that's blue), or an emerald (that's green)."

"Um, sapphire?" Hannah said.

"Oh, darn. I picked emerald," Emmie said. "I thought we might have the same Unicorn Reflection."

"Darn," Hannah said.

Emmie knew very well that Hannah was being sarcastic. She continued anyway.

"Last question. If you were on a desert island, would you want a book, television, or phone?" Emmie said.

"My phone, because it can be a book and television and also a phone... You know, so I can call people to tell them I'm lost on a desert island!" Hannah said.

Emmie nodded, then traced the vine to discover that Hannah was part of a different unicorn family: Moon Drops. Emmie knew about them from her previous reading. She knew that Moon Drops were the most mysterious unicorns. Her books knew very little about them, because they were rare and kept hidden. Hannah was a Moon Beam.

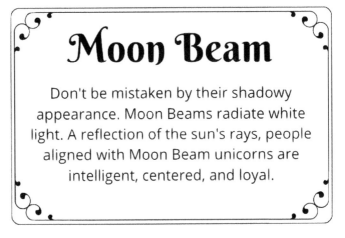

Moon Beam

Don't be mistaken by their shadowy appearance. Moon Beams radiate white light. A reflection of the sun's rays, people aligned with Moon Beam unicorns are intelligent, centered, and loyal.

"Wow," Hannah said.

She held out the single syllable for a long

time to appease Emmie and to simultaneously annoy Mom.

Mom side-eyed Hannah but then gave her a wink.

"Thanks for playing, Han," Mom said, relinquishing Hannah back to her retreat.

Hannah slinked upstairs, still sipping on her straw. Emmie slumped into her chair.

"What's wrong, Em?" Mom said.

"Hannah doesn't want to play with me anymore," Emmie said.

"She's just getting older, and her interests are changing. She'll want to play with you again soon."

Dad, who had been watching a football recap, chimed in.

"Your uncle and I used to be the same way, Emmie. I wanted to play with him, but all he wanted to do was listen to music in his room alone."

"What did you do?" Emmie asked.

"Well, it made me sad, too," Dad said. "But as we grew, our interests changed and sometimes intersected, and now we're best friends! When I think of it, he was the first friend I ever had. No one can take his place."

Emmie thought about it, and it made a lot of sense. Hannah was the first friend she ever had, and they would be friends forever, no matter what.

2

Accidental Unicorn

Emmie tried to keep Dad's story in mind whenever Hannah wouldn't play with her. She tried to remember that, one day, they would feel closer in age. Someday, they would be best friends. It was hard, though, because someday seemed very, very far away, and Hannah didn't help matters. Sometimes Emmie would shout it at Hannah when her older sister was being particularly snotty toward her.

"You'll be my best friend someday!" Emmie would say.

"Not today!" Hannah would reply. "Go away!"

Then Emmie would find herself standing on the wrong side of a locked door. Sometimes she'd pout, sometimes she'd cry, but mostly she'd shrug and return to her unicorn books. She knew her sister would need her one day, and she would be ready when that day came.

We'll be friends forever, no matter what, Emmie reminded herself.

As summer ended and the school year drew near, Emmie worried that she was losing her chance to hang out with Hannah. One rainy day, when they were both stuck inside, Emmie mustered up all of her courage and knocked on Hannah's door.

"Go away, Emmie," Hannah said.

It seemed as if Hannah had a security camera set up, so Emmie looked around.

What Emmie didn't know is that Hannah had learned her knock. It was heavy-handed but hesitant. Dad's knock, also heavy-handed, was more decisive. Mom's knock was a gentle double-knock-then-enter.

Emmie was still quietly looking for a camera when Hannah opened the door. They were both shocked to see the other. Emmie wrapped her arms around Hannah in a tight embrace. Hannah wiggled her way out of the hug.

"Stop, Emmie!" Hannah demanded.

Dad called from downstairs.

"Emmie Jo!" He warned.

"I was just hugging her, Dad!" Emmie said.

"Oh. Then carry on!" Dad said.

Emmie embraced Hannah once again.

"Dad!" Hannah yelled.

"Hug your sister, Hannie," Dad called back.

"Ugh," Hannah said.

She used her hand as a lever between herself and Emmie and pried her little sister away.

"Get. Off. Of. Me," she grunted.

Hannah broke free, and Emmie rubbed the spot on her arm where Hannah pushed.

"Do you want to play school?" Emmie asked.

"No, we go back to real school soon. I don't want to pretend I'm there already,"

Hannah said.

"Well, what do you want to play?" Emmie asked.

"Nothing."

"C'mon, Hannah! I want to play."

"Okay, how about a guessing game?" Hannah said.

"Yes!" Emmie said.

"I'm going to put my hand behind my back. If you can guess which number I'm holding up, I'll play with you for the rest of the day. Ready?"

Emmie nodded emphatically. Hannah put up three fingers.

"Um, three?" Emmie said.

"Nope," Hannah lied.

She added a finger.

"Um, four," Emmie said.

Hannah was surprised, but put down her ring finger and pinky.

"Nope! Peace out!" Hannah said.

She showed Emmie her two fingers, in the form of a peace sign.

"Hey! No fair!" Emmie said. "You cheated!"

"Did I?" Hannah asked.

"Probably!" Emmie said.

"We had a deal," Hannah said. "And you lost."

"Dad!" Emmie yelled.

"Hannah, whatever you're doing, stop doing it," Dad yelled.

"Why do you always assume it's me?" Hannah said.

She went back into her room, slammed the door, and locked it behind her.

Emmie knocked on the door, then knocked again, then started banging.

"Let me in!" she yelled.

"Emmie! That's enough!" Dad yelled.

He stormed over to the end of the staircase and looked up at Emmie, who was cross-armed and furious at the top of the stairs, outside of Hannah's room.

"But!" Emmie cried.

"To your room, Emmie!"

Emmie kicked Hannah's door, then went into her room and slammed her door, too. She put her back against the door and slid down it.

"I wish I had a different sister," Emmie said.

What Emmie didn't know is that Hannah was also sitting with her back against her own door.

"I wish I didn't have a sister," Hannah said.

The two remained in their rooms for the remainder of the evening. Emmie cried herself to sleep.

The next morning, Emmie awoke and met Mom and Dad downstairs for breakfast. She was still in her dress from the day before and wore her hippo slippers. She rubbed her dry eyes as she walked into the kitchen.

"Good morning, Emmie," said Dad.

"Good morning!" she chirped.

Emmie's eyes lit up when she saw the big stack of blueberry pancakes awaiting her. She had almost forgotten the fight until she realized Hannah wasn't in the kitchen. Mom noticed Emmie's search for her big sister.

"Hannah slept in today," Mom said.

Emmie nodded and took her seat. Emmie drowned her stack in maple syrup. She took a big bite. While her mouth was still full, she asked Dad if they could go to the zoo.

"Chew, Emmie," Dad cautioned.

She took a large swig of orange juice to wash down the pancake. She gulped then inhaled.

"Can we go to the zoo today?" she repeated.

"Let's keep an eye on the weather," Dad said. "As long as there's no rain, we should be able to go this afternoon."

Emmie wiggled in her seat. She had a happy dance that she did when she was, well, happy. It involved waving her hands to the left, then to the middle, then to the right, then back to the left, while she shook her hips back and forth.

Pancakes and the zoo? The day was off to a great start! It was definitely better than yesterday.

Mom and Dad cleaned the kitchen from breakfast as Emmie finished her plate. She rinsed her dish and put it into the dishwasher and thanked her mom for breakfast.

"Will you go wake your sister?" Mom asked.

"Are you sure you want me to wake her?" Emmie asked. She raised a brow at her mom, who chuckled.

"Yes, it will be fine," Mom said, then added, "Maybe also tell her that I asked you to get her."

Emmie nodded. She skipped up the stairs, despite her Mom's caution to walk, and headed straight into Hannah's room without knocking.

"Mom asked me to get—WHOA—"

Emmie fell back at what she saw in Hannah's bed. Four white hooves pushed through the lilac sheets, and two giant ears pointed against the pillow. Emmie slowly crept near the door, but carefully investigated the scene. The creature moved, and Emmie froze.

She heard a "Get out!" come from under the covers.

"What?" Emmie whispered.

"Get out of my room, brat!" the creature said.

It sat up in the bed, two front hooves slouched over two back hooves.

"Hannah?" Emmie asked, moving toward the creature.

"What do you want, Emmie?" the creature said.

"Um, Hannah. I think... You're a unicorn."

"It's too early for this," said the unicorn in Hannah's voice, a single spiral horn jutting from her forehead. She attempted to stand from the bed, but fell, making a loud THUD!

"Girls! Stop horsing around!" Dad called from downstairs.

More like "stop unicorning around!" Emmie thought.

"What the..." said the unicorn, unable to get up from the floor.

"You're not used to having four legs!" Emmie said.

"OMG, Emmie! I'm a horse!" Hannah said.

Emmie grabbed Hannah's mirror off of her desk.

"No, you're a unicorn!"

Unicorn Hannah took one look in the mirror, then fainted. Emmie ran downstairs, but once she saw her parents, she knew she couldn't tell them that their eldest daughter had been turned into a magical creature.

"Where's your sister?" Mom said.

"Um… She's not… feeling herself today," Emmie said. "I told her I'd bring her breakfast."

"Okay. I'll be up to check on her soon," Mom said.

"Uhm… okay…" Emmie said.

She grabbed a plate of pancakes and a glass of orange juice and ran upstairs. As she arrived at her sister's room, she found Hannah… erm… the unicorn version of Hannah awakening on the floor.

"What happened?" Hannah asked.

"Well… Don't faint again, but…"

Hannah looked at her hooves and back to the mirror, which Emmie dropped on the floor.

"It wasn't a dream?!" she squealed.

"Hannah, calm down," Emmie said. "We'll fix this."

"But, Emmie, I'm a horse!"

"Unicorn."

"Right. I'm a unicorn. I'm a unicorn?" Hannah squealed again.

Her eyes darted around the room as if she had been flooded with a million thoughts. She shook her head multiple times. Then she took a deep inhale and nodded.

"Emmie, you're the only one who can help me. You know all about unicorns."

Emmie smiled. It felt great that her sister needed her, and she knew just what to do. Emmie heard a familiar creaking of the fourth step from the top of the stairs, and Hannah's ear flicked. Hannah must've heard it, too.

"Oh, no! Mom's coming!" Hannah cried. "Help! She can't see me like this."

A soft tap-tap rattled the door, and then the door handle jiggled.

"Coming, Mom!" Emmie said.

She squeezed through the door into the hallway and shut it behind her.

"I was coming to check on Hannah. Is she feeling better?" Mom asked.

"She can't talk right now. She's a little… hoarse." Emmie said.

She'd never lied to her mom before, and she wasn't going to start now. It was true, Hannah was a little horse… with a horn.

Mom asked that Emmie let Hannah get some rest, but Emmie insisted Hannah wanted her help.

"It's okay, Mom." Hannah groaned from the bedroom. "Emmie can stay."

Mom looked suspicious, but she allowed Emmie to stay upstairs with Hannah.

"Just let me know if she gets a fever or anything or if you start to feel sick, too," Mom said.

Emmie nodded then returned to Hannah's room. Hannah was struggling to pick up the fork with no fingers or thumbs. She pawed at the fork and attempted to squish it between her two front hooves. Emmie couldn't help but chuckle as the unicorn that was once Emmie's sister gave up and started eating her food straight from the plate. She also lapped up the juice from the cup.

"Next time, I'll bring it in a bowl," Emmie said.

"I hope there is no next time. Let's try to have me back to human by lunch, okay?"

Emmie wasn't sure that was a promise she could keep, but she'd surely try. To get started, she'd need every unicorn book on her shelf. She snuck out of Hannah's room and tiptoed to her own.

Emmie grabbed every book that featured a horn, even a few dinosaur books, just for good measure. Then she returned to her sister's room. The nice thing about Hannah's hooves was that she wasn't able to lock Emmie out.

Emmie set down the books and spread them out across the bed. Next, she helped her sister get into a more comfortable position.

"Do you need anything before we get

started?" Emmie asked.

"No, let's just get this over with!" Hannah demanded.

Hannah was grumpy, and for the first time, Emmie understood why. Emmie realized it must've been scary for Hannah to wake up as a magical creature. It was scary for Emmie to wake up to a unicorn sister! Emmie used to think she'd give anything to be a unicorn, but seeing her sister sprawled out uncomfortably on her bedroom floor made Emmie think twice about that wish. Still, she didn't mind having a unicorn around.

"Okay, first we should determine what type of unicorn you are," Emmie said.

"I already took that dumb quiz," Hannah protested.

Emmie imagined that if she could, Hannah would be crossing her arms right now, but her long horse legs wouldn't allow it.

"No, no, silly! That was your Unicorn Reflection," Emmie explained. "We need to find out what actual unicorn you are."

Emmie licked her finger and flipped through the pages of *From Moon Drops to*

Star Shadows: A History of Unicorns until she found what she needed. It was a beautiful, two-page, full-color spread. The images were painted in pastel watercolors, and there were signs of nature around each unicorn, like autumn leaves, spring flowers, and glistening snowflakes. She studied the picture closely, then looked at Hannah, then back to the book, then back to Hannah.

"Well?" Hannah said.

"Based on your color, shape, and size, you're one of three unicorns."

Emmie pushed the book toward Hannah so she could see. The three unicorns that were small in stature with white coats were Icy Calliopes, Gemstone Wanderers, and Silver Starlights. Hannah inspected the book but wasn't able to get nearly as close, because her long snout got in the way. Emmie lifted it to help her.

"What about the horns?" Hannah said. "Each of these has a different color horn. Do any of them match mine?"

Emmie looked at Hannah's horn, it was a pale blue with silver sparkles throughout. The horn also swirled, like an ice cream cone. She looked back at the page and saw that the Icy Calliope had a white, almost translucent horn, while Gemstone Wanderer had a pinkish, geometric horn. She traced her finger to the Silver Starlight, her heart raced as she looked upon the horn, hoping it would be a match. Unfortunately, the horn of the Silver Starlight unicorn was, well, silver. It had no other distinguishing color. She shook her head and Hannah put her head down.

"Wait!" Emmie said. "I think I remember…"

She thumbed through the book. Hannah lifted her head in anticipation. Emmie pounded a fist of cheer into the air.

"Yes! I knew it!" Emmie said.

"What? What?" Hannah pleaded.

"There was another kind that wasn't listed on this page. It's a Crystal Dreamer. Yes! This is you!"

Emmie held up the page, which displayed a majestic Crystal Dreamer with its white coat and pale blue, shimmering horn. Emmie read the description of the Crystal Dreamer to

Hannah. Hannah's unicorn eyes were apparently just as capable of rolling back into her head when she was annoyed as her human ones had been.

"Crystal Dreamer. When a Crystal Dreamer comes to you in your slumber, she is there to remind you of what matters in life. Through dreams, she gently guides you along your path. Rarely, a Crystal Dreamer can… Uh-oh."

"What?" Hannah said. "Rarely a Crystal Dreamer can what?"

Emmie shook her head and closed the book. It couldn't be! Emmie simply wouldn't allow it.

"What? What is it?" Hannah pleaded.

"It said that sometimes a Crystal Dreamer could present herself as the person she visits. The person and the unicorn exchange forms. When this happens, the person has until sunset to return to her path, or else she'll be turned into a Crystal Dreamer… forever."

Hannah started to cry, and Emmie cried with her. At that moment, Emmie didn't think about how much she wanted to spend time with her big sister or about how cool it was to be in the presence of a majestic creature. She only thought about her new mission, which was to turn this unicorn back into Hannah.

3

Who Needs the Zoo, When You've Got a Unicorn?

"Do you want ice cream? I want ice cream."

Emmie spoke in a frantic, high-pitched tone. She paced the room.

"How can you think of ice cream at a time like this?" asked Hannah.

"I won't be able to think at all if I don't get some ice cream and fast!" Emmie said.

"Fine. Go get your ice cream. Just get back before sunset," Hannah said, half-jokingly. "And bring a bowl for me!"

Emmie went into the kitchen and pulled

down two blue bowls and got out the tub of strawberry shortcake. She noticed that the adults had a tub of butter pecan. This made her feel sad for all of the adults in her life. First, they had to work all day, then they lost their taste buds and enjoyed disgusting flavors of ice cream. Who would choose to eat butter pecan?

"Hi, Squirt," Dad said.

He startled Emmie, who dropped the ice cream tub. Dad helped her to clean up the mess, and she wondered why he wasn't lecturing her on her prelunch food choice.

"I was just coming to talk to you," Dad said. "I can't take you to the zoo today."

"Oh," Emmie said. "That's okay."

She fixed her eyes on the two empty bowls on the counter. She was disappointed, but she also knew that Hannah needed her more.

"So are you going to let me have this ice cream out of guilt?" Emmie asked.

"Yup," Dad said.

He laughed and scooped the strawberry shortcake into a bowl.

"Although I hope one of these bowls is for

your sister."

"It is!" Emmie said.

Dad scooped the second bowl and handed both to Emmie.

"Thanks for understanding about the zoo," he said. "I just got saddled with a lot of work."

"You may want to keep that saddle handy," Emmie mumbled under her breath.

"What?"

"Nothing! Gotta go!" Emmie said. "Thanks for the ice cream!"

She pushed past Dad and ran up the stairs into Hannah's room. She set the bowls of ice cream on the floor, then locked the door.

"Shoot!" she said. "I forgot the sprinkles!"

"Um, I think I can help you there," Hannah said.

She tipped her head and a colorful waterfall of sprinkles showered from her horn into the bowls. Reds and pinks and blues and greens flooded the bowls and melted into the ice cream. Emmie was both disgusted and amazed.

"Whoa! I didn't know you could do that!"

Emmie said.

"Me neither. I also didn't know I sneezed glitter, but…"

Hannah motioned to her side table, which was now covered in silvery-blue specks. It looked pretty cool, like a sparkly art project. Emmie brought her hands to her mouth and giggled.

"It's okay. You can laugh," Hannah said. "It's actually not too bad being a unicorn, as long as it's not for eternity."

She chuckled, and Emmie gave a nervous smile in return.

"What else do we know about the Crystal Dreamer? I'd like to eliminate any other surprises," Hannah said.

Emmie flipped through the pages until she found a full spread about the Crystal Dreamer. On the left page, there was a beautiful drawing on the unicorn with details about the unicorn's physical features. On the right page, there were facts about the personality, mission, and location of the Crystal Dreamer species.

Hannah nudged the book so she could see

it. Emmie traced the words with her fingers as she read.

Crystal Dreamer

Crystal Dreamers can be found wherever there are dreamers. For artists, they are the muse. For the broken, they are the glue. For the lost, they are the map. They are the Unicorn Reflection for those with a broken heart. Quiet and poised, they lead by example.

"We know that they have a white coat and a silvery blue horn, but this also says they are known for their long, shiny manes, and— whoa—a wingspan of four feet," Emmie read.

She focused her wide eyes on Hannah.

"Do you have wings?"

"Um... I'm not sure..." Hannah said.

With that, a giant, feathered wing sprouted out from her body. It grew and grew and grew until it knocked over Hannah's bedside lamp.

Emmie tried to catch the lamp, but it fell to the floor with a rattling bang.

"Oh no! Did it break?" Hannah said.

She tucked the wing against her body.

Emmie inspected the lamp and returned it to the table.

"No, it's fine, but maybe keep your wings to yourself for now," Emmie said, patting Hannah's side.

One of Hannah's unicorn ears perked up, then Emmie heard the familiar squeak of the staircase.

"Girls?" Mom said. "Everything okay?"

"Yeah, mom! We're just playing together," Hannah said.

"Okay, be careful!" Mom said.

The girls didn't breathe until they heard the stair squeak again as mom returned downstairs.

"That was a close call!" Emmie said.

"Maybe we should take this unicorn body for a spin, see what it really can do!" Hannah replied.

"But how will we get you out of the house without Mom and Dad seeing?" said Emmie.

Hannah nudged the book over to Emmie and smiled.

"Ohhhh, no," Emmie said. "You haven't even figured out how to walk as a unicorn and now you want to fly? Oh, no. No, no, no."

"Do you have a better suggestion?" Hannah said.

"Well, no," Emmie said.

"Then open that window, and hop on!" Hannah said.

Emmie gulped. She did as she was told but let her apprehensions be known the whole time she was doing it.

"Emmie, trust me. I would never put you in harm's way," said Hannah. "It's like the sprinkles. I just know I can fly. I can feel it."

Emmie exhaled and climbed onto Hannah's unicorn back. She was a small unicorn, so it wasn't nearly as difficult as mounting a horse or like playing horsey with Dad in the living room. Hannah was only slightly larger than that.

"Do you trust me?" Hannah said.

Emmie nodded and said, "Giddy-up!"

With that, Hannah raised her front hooves

and leaped. The two flew over Hannah's desk and out through the window.

Emmie took a deep breath as they glided above ground and soared toward the sky. Emmie couldn't believe her eyes. They were flying!

"Ow, Emmie, my hair!"

"Oops, sorry! I don't have anywhere else to hold on to."

Emmie wrapped her arms loosely around Hannah's long, equine neck.

Hannah flew them into the clouds so they wouldn't be seen by the neighbors. She imagined her mom getting that call: *Hi, I just saw your daughter flying on a unicorn!* Hannah and Emmie had enough excitement for one day. They didn't need their parents finding out about it, too.

Hannah didn't want to go too far, in case their parents got suspicious and looked for them in her bedroom. She flew them off of the property and into a nearby park. She knew there would be families and pets in the area, so she landed them gently within the shelter of an old weeping willow tree next to a large pond.

"WOO!" Emmie yelled when they landed. "That was awesome!"

"It actually was!" Hannah said. "I didn't know unicorns were so cool."

"I tried to tell you!" Emmie said.

She dismounted, and Hannah leaned back to stretch her front legs, then dropped her chest to the ground, then extended her back legs one at a time to *streeeetch*.

Emmie rested against the trunk of the tree and watched Hannah gallop around the ring of the weeping willow, sheltered by the long, draping leaves. Hannah reared up on her back legs and stretched out. It looked like a picture out of one of Emmie's books. When she returned to all fours, the unicorn took five trotting steps, shouted "Woo-hoo!" and then leaped into the air.

Emmie watched in awe as the unicorn's white coat appeared to change in color as she moved. It reminded her of an iridescent putty she once had. When she would move it in the light, the putty would change its silvery color to a metallic pink or blue or purple. The unicorn's coat did the same as the sun peaked through the willow's curtain of draping branches.

Emmie thought about the random facts about unicorns she had memorized through the years. She knew that Silver Starlights loved beets, Moon Drops lived off of potatoes, and Gemstone Wanderers ate nothing but coconuts. She also knew that, like dogs, all unicorns were allergic to chocolate, which she thought was sad. Emmie knew nothing about the diet of the Crystal Dreamer.

"I think I have an idea," Emmie said.

Hannah slowed her gallop and trotted over to Emmie.

"You've eaten ice cream and pancakes, but you haven't tried anything that unicorns would eat—like foods found in the wild."

"Um, is that safe?" Hannah said.

"Well, we won't know until we try," Emmie said.

At this point, Hannah was willing to try anything to be back to her normal self.

Emmie walked along the edge of the park, and Hannah stayed under the cover of the weeping willow. Emmie soon returned with a handful of tiny, red berries. Hannah gave her a look, but then ate them.

"Oh, hey! They're not too—blllllahhhh!"

A giant, colorful arc of liquid light spewed from her mouth and onto Emmie's lap. Hannah hadn't just thrown up. She'd puked a rainbow!

"Gross!" Emmie said.

She touched the glittery rainbow puke, which also shimmered like her iridescent putty—but slimier. Emmie decided that this was cooler than it was gross.

"Are you okay?" Emmie asked.

"Don't ever eat wild berries, Emmie. Ever," Hannah scolded.

She found a spot next to Emmie and curled up. After a moment, she felt better, but she and Emmie would never attempt to eat anything wild ever again.

"We should've brought real snacks," Emmie said.

"I could make some more sprinkles?" Hannah giggled.

She pointed her horn toward Emmie, and

Emmie shielded her eyes, expecting a waterfall of sprinkles. After a moment, she heard Hannah laugh. Emmie spread her middle and ring fingers so she could peek through her hands while keeping her eyes shielded. A giant bubble floated by.

Emmie unshielded her eyes and saw that she was enveloped in a sea of bubbles. Hannah had blown them through her horn!

Hannah laughed and blew bubbles straight in Emmie's face.

Emmie swatted them away, laughing. She stood up and chased the bubbles around, just like when they were little. She tried to catch them and twirled and twirled until she was dizzy and fell over laughing. Hannah reared on her hind legs and triumphantly blew more bubbles into the air.

Laughing with her big sister and sharing a secret—to Emmie, this was better than flying! In some ways, she wished the day would never end, but she did want her actual sister back.

Hannah stretched out under the weeping willow, and Emmie joined her. She had to resist the urge to cuddle and pet the unicorn lying next to her. Her sister was not a cuddler.

Hannah's ear perked up at a rustling from the other side of the tree.

"Someone's coming!" Hannah whispered, then disappeared.

"Hannah?" Emmie squealed. "Where are you?"

"You can't see me?" Hannah said.

Emmie jumped.

"No! You're invisible!"

A family walked under the willow at that moment. They were far enough from Emmie but close enough that they would've noticed a magical creature hiding beneath the tree. They continued to walk through the willow grove and didn't seem to notice Emmie perched against the trunk. Emmie watched them as they walked away.

"Since you're invisible, maybe we could go into town?" Emmie said.

"Oh, Emmie, I don't know. We need to figure this out!"

"Maybe we visit the bookstore and see if any of their unicorn books have the answer?"

Hannah reappeared. She thought about it for a moment, nodded, and then disappeared.

Emmie waved her hand in the air, trying to feel for the unicorn. She found the long, unicorn mane and grabbed ahold. Hannah guided her through the park and into town.

The sidewalks were bursting with people. Children tugged on their parents' shirtsleeves, as the adults juggled handfuls of shopping bags. People of all ages bumped into the invisible unicorn and apologized to no one, as

Hannah and Emmie waded through the bustling crowd.

Open shop doors released small puffs of air conditioning, beckoning hot bodies into the store. Emmie longed to step into any store to cool down, but Hannah was determined to find the bookshop. A gust of particularly cold air came from one store, catching Emmie's breath and attention.

"It's ice cream!" Emmie said.

Almost instinctively, Emmie turned toward the shop and walked toward the door.

"Not now, Emmie," Hannah said.

Before Emmie could respond, she realized she no longer had hold of Hannah's mane. She felt around in the air and bumped into an unsuspecting woman, who asked if she was lost and needed help.

"No, ma'am," Emmie said, then walked away.

She waited until she was far enough away from the helpful woman, then started whispering for Hannah. To ward off any other helpful adults, Emmie pretended she was looking for a lost dog.

"Hannah! Here, girl!" she called.

A few heads turned and looked down and around for a stray.

"Heeeeereee, Hannah! Here, girl!" Emmie called.

She had a pretty good idea where the bookstore was, so she headed in that direction. As she walked, she noticed a weird phenomenon on the ground: sprinkles in a direct line, as if they had been intentionally left on the sidewalk. At first, Emmie wondered if it was some marketing ploy from the ice cream shop, but then she remembered that her sister could shoot sprinkles from her horn. Hannah was leaving Emmie a trail to find her!

Emmie followed the trail, which led around a corner and down an alley. At the end of the trail, she found her sister with a horsey scowl on her face and her previously white mane drenched and muddy.

"What happened to you?" Emmie asked, stifling a laugh.

"Since no one can see me, some man tripped over me and spilled his iced latte,"

Hannah said.

Emmie couldn't contain it and burst into laughter.

Hannah exhaled. "You finished?" she said.

Emmie nodded, releasing putters of giggles.

"Okay, well, the bad news is when I have anything on me, I lose my invisibility. Luckily the man was too preoccupied by his phone to notice the unicorn he tripped over. So you need to find a way to wash me off before anyone else sees," Hannah said.

Emmie saluted Hannah as if to say aye, aye captain then rounded the corner. She returned with a large, plastic cup filled with water and poured it over Hannah.

Hannah, now even more annoyed, spit out the residual water.

"Refreshing."

For a drenched unicorn, Hannah's tone was cool and sarcastic. Emmie burst out laughing once again. Hannah shook herself off, like a dog after a bath. The water splashed Emmie, who laughed harder. Hannah nodded and rolled her eyes.

"Well it worked, didn't it?" Emmie asked.

Hannah disappeared at that moment. It did work! Hannah reappeared so that Emmie would find her wet mane.

"Hold on this time, and no ice cream!" Hannah said.

"Got it," Emmie said, through muffled giggles.

They walked back out onto the main sidewalk and continued their journey to the bookstore. This time, Hannah led them to the edge of the sidewalk, closer to the street. That way, her little sister wouldn't be tempted by the stores. They walked by a police officer on horseback. The uniformed officer was perched atop her brown horse. As the invisible unicorn led Emmie near the horse, the horse began to follow.

"Whoaaaa, girl," The police officer said.

The horse did not listen. It continued to follow Hannah and Emmie. The officer pulled on the reins, but the horse did not stop.

"Young lady, what are you doing?" the officer asked from atop the horse.

"Um, going to the bookstore," Emmie said.

"No, I mean to my horse. Are you feeding her?"

"No, ma'am."

"Are you teasing her?"

"No, ma'am."

Hannah stopped moving. As she did, Emmie stopped moving, and the horse stopped moving. As soon as Hannah started moving, Emmie and the horse followed.

"Oh, no, Emmie. It's me!" Hannah whispered. "The horse can sense me or maybe even see me!"

"Young lady! I must ask you to stop!"

Hannah stopped, Emmie stopped, and the horse stopped. The police officer dismounted and inspected Emmie. As she rounded her, she bumped into invisible Hannah, who grunted and moved away. The police officer said sorry, then turned to see no one near her. She turned back to Emmie with a look of confusion.

Emmie shrugged and smiled a wide, guilty smile.

"I don't know how you're doing it, but please stop."

"Honestly, I wish I knew how to attract horses this way! I would have one follow me home and keep it as a pet!" Emmie said.

"Okay, well, off you go."

Hannah pulled Emmie back toward the shops. The horse started to follow, but the officer pulled her back, and she was lost in the crowd behind them. Emmie held tightly on to Hannah's mane, so she wouldn't be lost too.

Back on their route to the bookstore, the sisters passed several more shops. Hannah stopped outside of one. Emmie looked at the sign and saw that it was a bubble tea shop that recently opened.

"Hey, no fair! I wasn't allowed to stop for ice cream, but you're stopping for bubble tea?" Emmie cried.

"Shush," Hannah whispered.

She didn't budge, just stood outside of the shop's large window.

Emmie wished she could see her sister to understand what they were doing there. She looked around and then through the window. The place was packed with families and preteens. A couple of girls sat at a two-seat high table nearest the window. Emmie recognized the girls immediately.

"It's Katie and Laney," Emmie whispered.

"Yes, I recognize my best friends, Emmie. Shhh," Hannah responded.

"Do you want to say 'hi' or something?" Emmie asked.

Hannah didn't respond. Emmie felt a drop of water on her hand.

"We better get a move on. I think it's raining," Emmie said.

She looked up. Another drop hit her hand, and then she heard sniffles. Hannah was crying.

"Hannah?" Emmie said. "Are you okay?"

"I'm fine," Hannah muttered.

Without realizing Emmie could hear her, Hannah muttered to herself, "We were supposed to go there together."

She started to pull Emmie back in the direction they came from.

"Where are we going? What about the bookstore?" Emmie asked.

Hannah didn't give a full response, just stormed off angrily. Under her breath, Emmie heard her say, "Home. I don't want to be a stupid unicorn anymore."

4

The Best Medicine

The flight home was quiet and less fun. It gave Emmie time to think about how Hannah must've been feeling at that moment. Emmie knew how it felt to be left out. She felt that way a lot when her big sister had friends over. She was sad that Hannah felt that way today, even worse that it may have been Emmie's fault that Hannah was changed into a unicorn. She regretted her wish for a different sister.

"That's it!" Emmie said as they landed in the backyard. "I wish Hannah was my sister again!"

The unicorn stared at Emmie, then slowly blinked.

"Huh?" Hannah said.

"Shoot. It didn't work," Emmie said.

"No, I guess not."

Hannah made herself invisible while they walked through the patio door into the living room.

"Emmie, I didn't know you were outside. I thought you were upstairs with Hannah," Mom said.

"She needed a nap, so I let her rest. I'll go check on her now."

"Maybe I should check on her, take her temperature," said Mom.

"No!" Emmie said.

Mom stopped and stared at her.

"I mean, she seems fine. Just needed some rest."

"Ohhhhkay," said Mom. "Just let me know if anything changes."

As Emmie and Hannah walked upstairs, they overheard Mom and Dad whispering.

"They seem like they're up to something," said Dad.

"I know, but they're getting along, and I don't want to ruin it," said Mom.

Emmie and Hannah could hear their parents chuckle as they reached Hannah's room.

Emmie felt Hannah push past her to enter the room, and the door shut between them. Emmie tried to open the door, but couldn't. Even though Hannah couldn't lock the door, the weight of her unicorn body held it shut.

"Hannah! Let me in!" Emmie said.

"Well, that didn't last long," Mom said from downstairs.

"Hannah!" Emmie said, pushing her shoulder against the door.

"No, Emmie. Go away!"

"But I need to help you," Emmie said.

"I don't want your help. Go away!" Hannah said.

"Emmie Jo!" Mom warned.

"Fine," Emmie said.

Once again, she kicked the door in protest. Upon entering her own room, she picked up a stuffed unicorn from her floor and threw it against the wall.

I never want to see another unicorn as long as I live, she thought.

She immediately took it back. She still loved unicorns, and she still loved her sister, but she felt hurt that, once again, Hannah pushed her away. Emmie crawled into her bed and began to cry. She pulled her stuffed dinosaur to her heart and snuggled it.

She rolled onto her back and stared at the ceiling through watery eyes. Her glow-in-the-dark stars soaked up the midday sunlight. She calmed herself by naming the constellations that Mom had assembled: Orion, Big Dipper, Little Dipper. Her eyes felt heavy, and she let them close as she exhaled. On her next inhale, an unusual scent of bubble gum wafted in through her open window.

Emmie opened her eyes and rubbed them several times. It wasn't the tears clouding her vision. Her bedroom ceiling had been replaced by the night sky! She looked down at her body and saw that where she was once resting on her bed, she was now floating on a cloud. Emmie tried not to make any sudden movements but propped herself up.

"You're safe," a voice echoed.

"Who—who's there?" Emmie stuttered.

A Crystal Dreamer, much like her sister-unicorn, floated into view.

Emmie gasped. She took note of the dark sky and feared that she had slept too long. Was it already past sunset? Was Hannah a unicorn forever? She had only closed her eyes for a moment!

"Have no worries here, dear friend!" the unicorn said.

"My sister?"

"Is perfectly safe. I'm visiting you in your dream, Emmie," the unicorn explained.

"But it's past sunset!" Emmie said.

"Only in your dream. I'm Penelope," said the unicorn. "Poppy for short."

"Hello. I'm Emmie. But I guess you knew that already since you're in my dream," Emmie said.

Poppy giggled and nodded.

"Can you help me?" Emmie said.

"I know what you're going through, and it is scary, but have faith in yourself, your sister, and your love for one another," Poppy said.

She moved through the night sky as if doggy-paddling in water.

"You'll be friends forever, no matter what," Poppy said.

"But I don't want her to be a unicorn forever," Emmie said.

"She won't be. I believe in you. Listen to your heart!" Poppy said.

A cloud shaped like a pig floated in front of Poppy, and Emmie moved her head to see around it. When the cloud had passed, Poppy was gone. The night sky was replaced by Emmie's ceiling stars, and she was once again resting safely in her own bed.

Listen to my heart. She thought. Her eyes, now dry, searched the room. The stuffed unicorn she had thrown earlier lay among a pile of dirty laundry. Her desk was messy with markers, construction paper, glitter, and glue. Her eyes stopped on the bookshelf. On the very top rested a purple-bound book. It was the first book on unicorns that Emmie had ever received, and she had completely forgotten about it. She stood up and tried to reach it, but she was too short. She pulled over her desk chair, but even standing on the chair, she couldn't reach the top shelf. She attempted to stand on tiptoes, but the chair wobbled beneath her, making her feel unsteady. Emmie knew what she needed to do.

Emmie marched to Hannah's room and burst through the door. In a flash, the unicorn disappeared. Emmie shut the door behind her, and Hannah reappeared.

"Get out," she muttered.

"I need your help," Emmie said.

Emmie could see even through her pony-like features, that Hannah was glaring at her.

"I found another unicorn book, but I can't reach it. You don't want to be stuck like this forever, do you?" Emmie said.

Hannah huffed, then stood up. She disappeared once again as she walked through the door. Once they were in Emmie's room, she reappeared.

"You're getting the hang of this unicorn thing," Emmie said.

Hannah exhaled deeply.

"What do you want?"

"I need you to help me get that book. Can you fly to it?"

"Not without destroying your room," Hannah said.

Emmie's room was smaller than Hannah's, and Hannah's four-foot wingspan would create havoc in here.

"Hmm… Can I stand on your back?" Emmie said.

"Will this book turn me back to myself?" Hannah said.

"Maybe?"

As Emmie said this, her voice went up in the end, making it clear to Hannah that Emmie had no idea what she was doing.

"Listen, it's worth a shot," Emmie said.

"Fine."

Hannah positioned herself by the bookshelf. Emmie stepped on her desk chair, then onto Hannah's back. Hannah grunted.

"Stop moving," Emmie demanded.

"I'm not moving. You're sliding on my muscles. I'm not a step-stool, Emmie."

Emmie braced herself on the bookshelf and reached for the book. It was still too high, so she went onto her tiptoes again. She stumbled forward and almost fell off of Hannah's back. As she did, she heard the creak of the staircase.

"Oh, no!"

"Emmie, do you know where Hannah is? She's not in her room?"

Dad's voice came from around the corner. He entered the room to find his youngest child dangling from the bookshelf. Hannah had disappeared, so Dad couldn't see that Emmie was standing on the unicorn.

"EMMIE!" Dad cried. "What are you doing?"

He rushed over and nearly tripped on Hannah, who let out a small yelp. Dad grabbed Emmie from the shelf and placed her on the floor.

"What were you thinking?" Dad said.

"I couldn't reach my book," she said.

"You should've asked for my help," Dad said. "You scared me!"

"I'm sorry, Dad."

Dad squeezed her, and she snuggled into his arms.

"Did you have a good day with Hannah? Seems you two had a lot of quality time today," Dad said.

"Mm-hm."

"Where is she anyway?"

"Um…" Emmie said.

Just then, she heard the shower running. Hannah must've snuck out in all the commotion and hid in the bathroom.

"She's taking a shower," Emmie said.

"Okay, Mom or I will check on her in a little bit. Which book do you need?" Dad said.

Emmie pointed to the purple book on the top shelf, and Dad grabbed it for her. He turned it over and inspected the cover.

"Ah, yes, this old classic!" he said and handed Emmie the book.

She thanked him and he left, shutting the door behind him. Emmie waited until Dad was fully downstairs, then she rushed to the bathroom.

"The ghost is clear!" Emmie said.

The shower turned off, and the bathroom door opened. An invisible Hannah said, "It's 'the *coast* is clear.'"

"Oh. Well, it's safe to come out," Emmie said.

She followed Hannah back to her room, and Hannah reappeared.

"I'm sorry about earlier," Hannah said. "I just needed some time alone."

"I understand," Emmie said.

"I just don't want to be a unicorn forever. It made me sad to know that my friends were going to be doing fun stuff without me, and they'll never hang out with me again if I have to use a trough at the bubble tea shop."

"I'd still be your friend," Emmie said.

She put her arm around her sister-unicorn.

"Thanks, Emmie."

"I know how it feels to be left out," Emmie said. "It hurts."

"Do you feel like that a lot?" asked Hannah.

Emmie nodded, and Hannah looked down.

"Sorry," she muttered.

After a moment of silence, Emmie pulled out the purple book. The title, embossed in a gold script read *Spectacular Sightings: Angels to Zombies*.

"What does that have to do with me?" Hannah asked.

"I remembered there is a story in this book about a girl's sister being turned into a unicorn!"

Emmie traced her finger down the table of contents until she found the chapter entitled "The Accidental Unicorn," which was on page 55. She licked her finger and turned the pages.

"It's gross that you do that," Hannah said.

"It's super unhygienic."

Emmie rolled her eyes, and her sister once again muttered a sorry.

On page 55, there was a drawing of a little girl, no older than Emmie, standing next to a small unicorn. It was almost as if the drawing was of her and Hannah! She slid her fingers over the words as she read aloud:

The Accidental Unicorn

This spectacular sighting is different from the others, because it was not necessarily a sighting of a mystical creature but, instead, a transformation of a typical human into a majestic unicorn. The story of the accidental unicorn takes place in 1823, in the United Kingdom. For those less familiar with the unicorn species, Crystal Dreamers may appear anywhere there are dreamers. So it is not unusual for them to appear in countries around the world. What is unusual about this sighting is that the Crystal Dreamer didn't appear within a dream, as she usually does.

This Crystal Dreamer appeared within the body of a young girl. It is the first known instance of transformia unicornis, when a human is transformed into a unicorn.

Fourteen-year-old Marlow Cordin, of Ashwell, Hertfordshire, a quaint town outside of London, went to bed after a terrible fight with her younger sister Janine (age 8). When Marlow awoke the next day, her short black hair had been traded in for a long, white mane, and her body had been changed into that of a horse. The most identifying of features was the horn that had sprouted from her head and the four-foot wingspan that had grown overnight. Janine, a lover of mystic and magic, had read lore about Crystal Dreamers, but in none of her research had she read that Crystal Dreamers could inhabit human bodies.

The sisters tried everything to return Marlow to her human form. What the two didn't know is that time was not on their side. We've since learned, through a few unfortunate circumstances, that the inhabited person must make things right by sunset or else remain a unicorn forever.

Luckily, the sisters did not hesitate. They worked together as a team to undo the magic. They attempted to eat berries and leaves picked from the forest, but that led to a disaster of rainbow proportions.

"Been there…" Hannah commiserated.

"Shh!" Emmie said, then continued reading.

They visited a local witch doctor, but her incantations only made Marlow more magical. Nothing they did seemed to work.

Unbeknownst to the sisters, as the night drew close, Marlow was running out of time. As they watched the sunset over the valley, Marlow slowly returned to her human form. In a rare interview, Janine was asked how they broke the spell.

"You know what they say: Laughter is the best medicine." She spoke nothing more on the subject.

There are only a handful of known instances of transformia unicornis. Of those with happy endings, their way out of the spell remains a mystery.

"That's it?" Hannah cried. "Laughter is the best medicine?"

"I guess so," Emmie said.

It felt like her stomach was twisting into a giant knot. She knew she got her sister's hopes up, and all this did was remind them both of the looming deadlines.

"But we *have* laughed today, and I'm still a unicorn!" Hannah said.

"Maybe we have to laugh at the sunset?" Emmie said.

"Do we really want to wait until then to find out if that works?"

"No, I guess not," Emmie said.

Hannah stood up. She had a look of determination in her giant, adorable eyes.

"If it's laughter they want, it's laughter they're gonna get."

As Hannah made this proclamation, she disappeared and the bedroom door opened.

"Hannah! Where are you going?" Emmie whispered.

"To get some laughs."

5

Make 'Em Laugh

Emmie tried her best to follow Hannah, but an invisible sister was difficult to track. She extended her arms and felt around the air, trying to grasp hold of Hannah, but her sister was moving too fast. She grabbed a throw blanket from Hannah's bed and tossed it toward the stairs. The blanket clung in the shape of a unicorn on the steps. The unicorn-shaped blanket froze.

"Hey!" Hannah yelled.

"Sorry! I couldn't see you," Emmie whispered.

"Excellent. Now I can't see anything," Hannah said.

Emmie pulled the blanket off of Hannah, and the unicorn shape disappeared.

"Just meet me in the basement," Hannah whispered.

Emmie followed behind her sister as closely as she could. When she reached the basement, the door popped open, as if by a gust of wind. Emmie rushed over and headed down the stairs.

The Buttons' basement was finished with hardwood floors, a large area rug, cozy couches, a big-screen television, and giant beanbag chairs. Hannah's beanbag was navy blue and made of velvet. Emmie's was fuzzy and purple. Sports banners and football jerseys were framed and hung on the white walls, next to a shelf of trophies. When the basement wasn't in use for hosting game nights and sports viewings, it was converted into a preteen palace for movie nights and sleepovers.

Out of sight of their parents, Hannah reappeared and immediately began doling out orders. Emmie did as she was instructed, setting up the TV, picking the perfect movie, and dimming the lights. There were no windows in the basement, making it the ultimate movie theatre experience.

Emmie returned upstairs, placed a bag of popcorn in the microwave, and grabbed two sodas.

Dad gave her an inquisitive look. He hadn't seen Hannah walk downstairs, and he asked whether Emmie was planning to drink the two sugary drinks by herself, which was absolutely not allowed.

Emmie promised that Hannah would be joining her shortly. She crossed her heart to show him that she was telling the truth.

Dad smiled and offered to help her take the items down to the basement.

Emmie almost accepted the offer but remembered that her sister was a unicorn and didn't want Dad to see her.

"I've got it, Dad!" she said.

Dad watched in amusement as Emmie attempted to juggle the sodas, bowl, and popcorn bag by herself. He pulled down a wooden tray with metal handles and slid it across the kitchen island to her.

Emmie thanked him, and he winked. She balanced the bowl, popcorn bag, and sodas on the tray and headed to the basement door, which was shut. She huffed when she got there.

"Daaaad…" she sang.

Dad let out a small chuckle and jogged to the door to open it for her. He asked one more time if she needed any additional help, and she shook her head. Then she carefully stepped down the stairs, with the teetering tray.

She took it one stair at a time. At the bottom step, Emmie felt a sense of achievement, like a gymnast dismounting the balance beam. "Aaah," she sighed in relief.

Emmie set the tray between the beanbag chairs and settled into hers. She poured the popcorn into the big bowl and opened the sodas, slipping a reusable straw into each can.

Hannah dipped her snout into the bowl and chomped on a few pieces of popcorn.

Emmie sneered. She'd forgotten about the

unicorn's lack of opposable thumbs and wished she had gotten her sister a separate bowl... or a feedbag. She decided she would eat from only one side of the large bowl, to avoid her sister's slobber. She internally congratulated herself on the forethought to grab the straws for the soda. This made it easier for Hannah to sip the drink without help. The two sisters cozied up in their beanbags and started the movie. A familiar logo lit up the screen.

"Is this what I think it is?" Hannah asked.

Emmie shrugged coyly. When they were little, Emmie and Hannah cherished the movie *Frozen* and loved to sing along with the catchy tunes. They each chose a favorite character, dressed as her, and memorized all of her lines. It was one of Emmie's favorite memories with Hannah, and with its themes of sisterhood, Emmie thought it would be the perfect flick for their sister day.

"Oh! I haven't seen this in so long!" said Hannah.

They laughed and laughed through all the jokes and giggled as they sang along. They hadn't watched the movie together in years, but they still remembered all the lines and all of their favorite songs. They even split into the respective parts that they had chosen as little ones. Hannah sang to Emmie while smiling and acting out her part.

Emmie was having a blast! It felt great to be included in the fun. This was the best day she had had with her big sister in a long time. Still, she couldn't help but wonder if this was working to reverse the unicorn spell. She snuck a peek at her sister and was saddened to see that she was still a unicorn.

At the end of the movie, Hannah looked at her hooves and came to the same realization. Laughing through the movie had done nothing to help her break the spell.

"I forgot how sad that movie can be," Hannah said.

"Yeah, I feel sad when the sisters fight," Emmie said.

"Me too," said Hannah and put her hoof on Emmie's hand.

Emmie thought about the movie and about how the sisters' love for one another saved the day. She hoped her love would save her sister.

Hannah's ear perked up at the sound of a door opening, and on cue, she disappeared.

Shortly, Dad walked down the stairs.

"Emmie Jo…" he said.

"Yes, Daddy?" she said.

"Where's your sister?"

"I'm in here, Dad!" Hannah's voiced called from the basement bathroom.

Emmie was amazed at how fast Hannah was getting at covering her tracks.

"Oh, Han, you must've snuck by me!" Dad yelled through the bathroom door. "How are you feeling?"

"Much better! Just getting some quality time with Emmie today!" she said.

"Awesome! You girls have fun! Let me know if you need anything," Dad said.

He gave Emmie a thumbs up before heading back upstairs.

"The coast is clear!" Emmie said through the bathroom door.

It swung open, and the unicorn-that-was-once-Emmie's-sister reappeared.

"Ready for phase 2?" Hannah said.

"YES!" Emmie shouted. Whatever it was, Emmie was glad to be part of it. "Um, what is phase 2?" she asked.

"More laughter!"

"Another movie?" Emmie suggested.

"Nope! Follow me, but be very quiet," Hannah demanded.

When they reached the top of the stairs, Hannah said, "You stay and watch from here. I think you're going to love this!"

Hannah opened the basement door, then disappeared.

Emmie sat on the second stair from the top and used the top stair as cover. She hid behind it and peaked her eyes over it. The problem was that she wasn't sure where to look because Hannah was now invisible. She peered around the living room, searching for the comedy promised by her big sister.

Emmie could see Dad sitting on the couch, watching the sports channel. He yelled at the screen, making suggestions to the team's quarterback.

Suddenly, the channel switched to a kid's

show.

Dad jumped up. He made a *hmm* then looked for the remote, which had been secretively moved to the kitchen island, far across the room.

"Weird," Dad said to himself.

He retrieved the remote, changed the channel back to football, and set the remote on the sofa's arm. Once he had settled back into his game, Hannah went back to her silly prank.

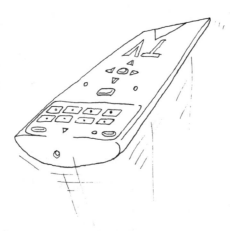

Emmie gasped as the remote levitated in the air. She had to cover her mouth to muffle her giggle. She knew exactly how this was happening: An invisible Hannah was sneakily moving the remote and changing the channel.

Dad was so enthralled in his show that he didn't notice the remote flying through the air to the island again. Hannah changed the channel back to a kid's show. Dad huffed and reached for the remote on the arm of the sofa, but it wasn't there. He looked around and then under the sofa and removed the cushions. He was baffled and started to say some words that no one in the house was allowed to say.

Emmie could hardly contain her laughter. She had to keep ducking behind the stair so she didn't attract attention to herself.

Dad looked to the island and saw the remote in the place he found it before. He grunted, stood up, and stormed over to the island to retrieve the naughty remote. Once again, he changed the channel and settled back into his seat.

Emmie caught her breath from laughing.

After Dad was comfortably watching his show, the remote once again levitated from the sofa, but this time, Hannah took the remote to the arm on the other end of the couch. When she changed the channel, Dad was beside himself.

He looked around the sofa again, then marched to the island. When it wasn't there, he scratched his head. He looked all around the room, then finally found the remote on the other end of the sofa.

"What in the world?" Dad said.

At this point, Emmie was laughing so hard that she had to go back into the basement so as not to be heard.

Hannah joined her and let out a huge *haaaahaaa*. It bellowed out of her as if she had been holding it in the entire time.

Emmie laughed so hard that she fell from the couch and couldn't get back up. The sisters were rolling on the floor when Dad yelled downstairs.

"Girls?" he said.

"Yes, Dad?" the girls said in unison.

"Were you just upstairs?"

"Nope," Emmie said.

She wasn't lying.

"Weird. Very weird," Dad muttered to himself.

The girls burst into even more laughter. It

felt good to have a special secret together, one that didn't involve Emmie's sister turning into a unicorn… well, mostly. When the laughs became chuckles that became giggles that became intermittent coughs, the girls caught their breath. Hannah exhaled one final giggled and turned to Emmie.

"I feel a little bad, though," Hannah said.

"Me too. Poor Dad," Emmie said.

"He only watches his sports on the weekends, and we ruined it," Hannah said.

"It was funny, though," Emmie said.

Hannah started laughing again, and Emmie did, too.

"But maybe that's the key. We can't do something that makes us laugh and makes us feel bad—like the movie made us laugh but also made us sad. Pranking Dad made us laugh, but made us feel a little guilty," Emmie said.

"Emmie, you're right!" Hannah said.

She thought for a moment, then perked up. It was as if Hannah had been holding on to a bunch of prank ideas that she never had the opportunity to use.

"I've got the perfect plan for phase 3," she said.

Hannah asked Emmie to go into Mom's craft room, find as much bubble wrap as possible, then meet back in the living room. Mom kept a lot of gift wrapping and shipping supplies in her craft room closet, so Emmie knew exactly what to do.

When she met Hannah in the living room, bubble wrap in hand, Emmie saw that Dad was no longer watching the TV. Her stomach knotted up as she felt a bit guiltier for ruining his weekend relaxation. She reminded herself it was for a good cause. They needed to save Hannah!

Hannah nudged the large area rug with her snout and asked for Emmie's help. Together, they rolled the rug up enough to set the bubble wrap under it. Then they covered the bubble wrap with the rug.

"Now, we wait," Hannah said.

The two went back to their perch at the top of the basement staircase. Hannah's horsey body barely fit on the step. She braced herself against the wall. Emmie wasn't sure what they were waiting on or why the plan involved bubble wrap, but when Mom entered the room, she found out.

Mom moved Hannah's jacket from a chair and hung it in the coat closet then went into the kitchen to pour a glass of iced tea.

"C'mon!" Hannah whispered.

"What?" Emmie said.

"Shhh," Hannah warned.

Mom crossed into the living room and POP! POP! POP! As Mom stepped on the area rug, the bubble wrap popped beneath her feet. Mom yelled and lifted her foot high into the air. As she set it down, Emmie heard a POP! POP! again and Mom lifted her other foot. She looked like she was walking around a pit of creepy crawlies, trying not to step on anything. The more she tried to sneak away from the popping, the more she popped.

"Eek!" Mom yelled.

She darted across the rug, popping as she went. Hannah and Emmie couldn't contain their laughter. Mom looked under the rug and pulled out the bubble wrap. The girls ran downstairs.

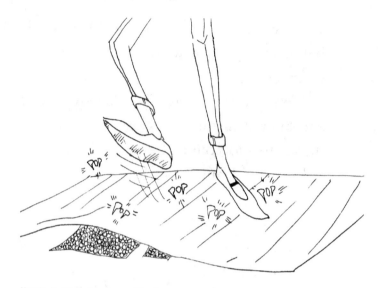

"Girls!" Mom called.

"Yes, mom?" the girls replied in unison.

"Okay, okay, you got me!" she said, laughing.

Emmie and Hannah laughed even harder than when they had pranked their Dad. They muffled their laughter when they heard Dad talking to Mom upstairs.

"Oh, the girls pulled a little prank on me," Mom explained.

"You know, they pulled a fast one on me today, too!" he said. "I don't know how, but I know it was them!"

"At least they're working together?" Mom

reasoned.

Knowing they weren't going to get in trouble, the girls continued their laughter. Emmie looked at her sister but saw she was still a unicorn. She stopped laughing.

"What's wrong?" Hannah said, her laughter slowed.

"You're still a unicorn," Emmie said.

"Oh."

Hannah stopped laughing.

"Phase 4?" Emmie asked.

"I'm out of ideas, Em." Hannah looked down.

Emmie looked down, too. She was also out of ideas, and it was almost dinnertime. Sunset wasn't too far away. Still, they had some time left, and Emmie wasn't going to let her sister remain a unicorn forever.

"We'll figure it out," Emmie said. "I promise."

6

Unicorn Princess

Last year, on Hannah's twelfth birthday, after all of the presents were unwrapped and the cake was eaten, Emmie asked Hannah to play "Unicorn Princess." This was a game that Hannah made up, where they both pretended to be unicorns searching for a tiara hidden within the house. Mom or Dad would hide the tiara and give them clues. Whoever found the tiara became the Unicorn Princess. Hannah almost always won. After a while, though, she'd let her little sister wear the tiara and be the princess, too.

However, the moment Hannah turned twelve, she gave Emmie the tiara and vowed to never play Unicorn Princess again.

"Why not?" Emmie whined.

"Because I'm not a unicorn," Hannah explained.

"But, but… It's just make-believe," Emmie said.

"I'm twelve now, and I don't play make-believe anymore."

"But you can!" Emmie said.

"No, I can't. When you turn twelve, your imagination disappears forever!" Hannah said.

"No, it doesn't!" Emmie cried.

"It's gone," Hannah insisted.

"But it can't be gone. It doesn't just go away."

"Yes, it does, and it has," said Hannah.

Emmie crossed her arms and looked up at her big sister through furrowed brows.

"So what do you see when you close your eyes?" she asked.

She watched as Hannah grabbed a penlight from Emmie's doctor kit. Hannah shined the light in Emmie's face.

"Close your eyes. What do you see?" Hannah said.

"Nothing. Just a big bright light," Emmie said.

"That's what I see when I close my eyes, except when I open them there's no one there with a flashlight," Hannah said.

She turned off the light and replaced it in the doctor kit.

"That's what happens when you turn twelve; you blow out the candles, and your imagination goes away with the smoke."

Emmie had been fearing her twelfth birthday ever since.

Now, just short of a year later, Emmie found herself in a real-life game of Unicorn Princess! Instead of trying to find a tiara, they were trying to find a counterspell. She left Hannah and wandered around her bedroom, as if in search of clues. How she wished Mom and Dad were in on the game to give them some clues this time!

"Crystal Dreamers always appear to people during their sleep. Do you remember what you dreamt about last night?" Emmie asked.

"Nothing about unicorns," Hannah said, defeated.

"But do you remember anything from your dreams?" Emmie pressed.

"Just a dream about a crown. It was hidden and I needed to find it. I could sense it somewhere in the dark, and it was pulling me to it like a magnet," Hannah said.

Emmie thought about her visit from the Crystal Dreamer, everything they had read, and Hannah's dream. She tried to piece everything together. Certain themes encircled her thoughts: guiding path, make things right, families, crown, sisters. Crown. Sisters. Path.

"OMG. Hannah! I've got it!" Emmie said.

She sat straight up. Hannah perked up and waited while her sister worked out the remaining details.

"We need to play Unicorn Princess!" Emmie said.

Hannah slumped down and rested her head.

"C'mon!" Emmie said.

Emmie began pushing her from behind. She did not budge.

"Are you telling me that every sister pair with the same Crystal Dreamer fate has played Unicorn Princess? It's a game that I made up!" Hannah said.

"No! Don't you get it? You need to follow your path, search for your crown! Mom and Dad put away the tiara last year. We need to find it!" Emmie insisted.

Hannah let out an annoyed grunt. They were running out of time, and this seemed like something that would just waste it further. Still, it was the first lead they had in a couple of hours, so it was worth a shot.

"Fine, but we have to be quick. Dinner is in an hour, and I need to be Hannah again or mom is going to flip!"

Emmie did her happy dance. Of course, she was hopeful that this would save her sister, but she was also excited to get to play her favorite game with Hannah again. She reminded Hannah of the rules: They both pretended to be unicorns (of course, Hannah had an advantage this time), and the first sister to find the tiara was the Unicorn Princess.

Hannah agreed, then disappeared. The

game was on!

Emmie went into her bedroom and dug through her toy chest. She knew the tiara wasn't in there, but she needed one item to help her get into the mindset for Unicorn Princess. She needed her unicorn horn headband. It was a beautiful, sparkly headband with ribbons down the side and a giant, stuffed unicorn horn on top. She looked in the mirror and placed the headband on her head. Emmie fancied herself with the horn. She brushed her long hair around it, while admiring herself in the mirror.

BANG! A crash came from the attic, startling Emmie and reminding her that the game was on. Hannah must be in the attic! It gave Emmie the idea of where she should check next. She rushed down the stairs, through the living room, and out to the garage.

The garage was organized with tall shelves that held large storage tubs. The tubs were slightly see-through but cloudy enough that a tiara couldn't be seen. Emmie pulled down the first tub and started digging.

Mom peeked her head out of the garage.

Emmie froze. Busted. She slowly turned her head toward Mom and smiled sheepishly. Her arms were still elbow-deep in a holiday tub, filled with wreaths made of colorful bulbs, pastel eggs, and plastic pumpkins.

"Oh! Unicorn Princess?" Mom said.

Emmie nodded.

"You're not going to find it in here!"

The first clue! Emmie sealed the lid onto the tub and slid the tub back on the shelf. She rushed by Mom on her way inside and thanked her for the clue.

Mom smiled. "Good luck!" she said.

Emmie stood in the living room. It was an open floor plan with airy shelving. There was no place a tiara could've been hidden for a year without Emmie noticing. She also knew it wasn't in the kitchen. She has been in every cabinet, nook, and fridge compartment in that room and never saw a tiara there. Hannah must've been right. It must've been put away in the attic.

Emmie ran upstairs and then up through the tiny crawl space that led to the attic. This was an unfinished space, it was hot and filled with spider webs, and Emmie did not want to be there too long. When she made it to the top, she saw that the light was off and Hannah was no longer there. Unless Hannah had already found the tiara, this was not the hiding spot. Emmie turned off the light and ran as fast as she could toward the light at the end of the stairs.

"Ew, ew, ew!" she cried as she ran through a sticky spider web.

As she neared the hallway, she could hear Dad talking to someone. Who was it? Then Emmie heard Hannah's voice. Had Hannah found the tiara? Did it change her back to her human form?

Emmie rushed toward the voices, which were coming from Hannah's room. Dad was standing in the doorway, but Hannah was nowhere to be found. Emmie snuck her head under Dad's arm, which was propped against the doorframe. She searched the room for Hannah and didn't see her.

"I already told Hannah it's not in here, but she refuses to come out from under her bed,"

Dad said.

Emmie gasped and looked under Hannah's bed but saw no one.

"Thanks, Dad, but I… don't want to use clues anymore because… I'm too old?" Hannah said.

Her voice went up at the end as if she was asking, not telling. Emmie realized it was because Hannah was politely trying to get Dad to leave the room. Hannah must've been invisible, meaning that she was still a unicorn.

"I heard the crash in the attic, so I came to check on you girls. When I got up here, I saw Hannah's unicorn horn poking around her room and knew it must be time for Unicorn Princess!" Dad said.

"You saw her horn?" Emmie asked.

"My headband, Emmie! He saw my unicorn headband," Hannah insisted.

Ohhhh.

"Right, her headband. Not a real horn, of course. That would be silly. Just a regular girl with a silly old headband on her head, not a real unicorn. Nope. Nothing to see here," Emmie rambled.

Dad gave her a confused look. Emmie couldn't stop talking.

"Just a regular girl. Regular headband. Not a unicorn."

"We get it, Emmie. I'm a human, wearing a headband. Why aren't you searching for the tiara?" Hannah called from somewhere in her room.

"Um, right!" Emmie said. "Dad, a clue?"

She pulled Dad toward her room so that Hannah could escape. He told her that she was getting warmer. She looked around her room. How could it be hiding in there for a year and she never saw it?

Dad laughed.

Emmie looked up from the pile of laundry she was sorting through. She scrunched her face at her laughing Dad.

"This may be a Unicorn Princess where the two of you have to work together," Dad said.

He shrugged and left the room.

That was it! The sisters needed to work together to break the spell! Emmie ran into Hannah's room.

"Hannah?" she whispered. "Hannah, where are you?"

"I'm in here!" Hannah called from Mom and Dad's room.

Emmie ran in to meet her. She was getting winded and a bit dizzy from all the running. She rested her hands on her knees, bent over, and caught her breath.

"Oh, stop being dramatic," Hannah said.

Emmie inhaled and then said, "We need to work together to break the spell!"

"I think you're right, Emmie," Hannah said. "What was Dad's clue?"

Emmie squinted at Hannah, trying to determine whether this was just some trick so that Hannah would win the game. Hannah realized Emmie didn't trust her at the moment and said, "Fine. Dad's clue to me was that I needed to cool down."

"Weird. Dad told me I was getting warmer," Emmie said. "Could it be the oven?"

"No, it would've melted by now. Maybe the freezer?"

"After all the times I snuck ice cream out of there, I would've seen it by now!" Emmie said.

"It must be something that can change from hot to cold," Hannah said.

"The bathtub?"

"OMG, Emmie. I know what it is!" Hannah said, then disappeared.

"Hannah! We're supposed to work together!" Emmie said.

"We did, Emmie! Come on!" Hannah said.

She started singing so that Emmie could follow the sound of her voice. They marched downstairs, through the living room and down into the basement. The singing stopped when Emmie reached the bottom of the stairs. Her Dad was on the couch, waiting for them.

"Where's your sister? I told you to work together!" he said.

"We did! She's—um—on her way," Emmie said.

A whistle came from around the corner. It was loud enough to catch Emmie's attention but quiet enough that Dad didn't hear. Emmie snuck away and met Hannah on the other side of the wall. She explained that Dad wasn't leaving and he was waiting on Hannah.

"It's in the safe! He has to open it for us." Hannah said.

"The safe? How is that hot and cold?"

"Because it's right below the thermostat!" Hannah said.

Oooohhh! Emmie hoped one day she would be as smart as her sister.

"But how do we get it? Dad won't open it until we're both in the room," Emmie said.

"I have an idea," Hannah said.

She crept around the corner and disappeared again.

"Dad?" Hannah called. "I need to go back upstairs. We figured it out. It's the safe under the thermostat. Will you open it for Emmie? She should be the Unicorn Princess this time!"

"But you need to wear the tiara!" whispered Emmie.

"I know. Just meet me in my room with it!" Hannah said.

Emmie rounded the corner and smiled at Dad.

"Well, I was hoping you'd both be here, but as long as you worked together!" Dad said.

Emmie nodded.

Dad entered the code for the safe, and the door popped open. Inside, among a pile of documents and loose items, was the tiara.

Emmie clapped.

Dad laughed and put the tiara on Emmie's head.

She was finally the Unicorn Princess. Oh, no! But she wasn't supposed to be the Unicorn Princess. In all the excitement, she almost forgot that Hannah needed the crown to break the spell!

"Thanks, Dad! Gotta go!" Emmie said, then ran upstairs.

She met Hannah in her bedroom. The unicorn-that-once-was-Emmie's-sister was draped across the bed. She looked defeated. Emmie presented her with the tiara and put it over the unicorn's horn. Nothing happened.

"Go figure," Hannah said.

She rolled over and curled her horsey body into a ball.

"Maybe we did something wrong? Or maybe we have to say something?" Emmie reasoned.

She paced the room.

"Or maybe... it's because I put it on," Emmie said.

She stopped pacing. She didn't sit or move. She simply stood in place, then started to cry.

"Emmie, I'm sure it's not because you put on the tiara. I'm sure this tiara had nothing to do with it at all," Hannah said.

Emmie stopped crying, sat on the edge of the bed, and looked at her sister.

"Besides, we now have another problem. It's about to be dinnertime, and I'm still a unicorn. How are we going to explain my absence at dinner?" Hannah asked.

Emmie wiped her eyes with her shirtsleeve and sniffled.

"You leave that to me," she said.

Emmie grabbed a few pillows and a blanket and headed downstairs.

7

First and Forever

Emmie marched into the kitchen and right up to Mom, who was pouring herself some ice tea. Emmie took notice that no one was cooking dinner. Usually, by this time, one of her parents would be zipping around the kitchen, chopping vegetables, and shaking skillets. She cleared her throat to get Mom's attention.

Mom looked at Emmie, then at the pile of bedding in Emmie's arms, and raised a brow.

"Mom, me and Hannah—"

"Hannah and I," Dad corrected from the living room.

Emmie rolled her eyes, huffed, and continued.

"Hannah and I were wondering if we could have a picnic in the basement as part of our sister day?"

Emmie made her eyes as large as a puppy's and gave a little pout with her lips. "Pleeeeease!" she said.

Mom chuckled. "You don't have to give the puppy dog eyes, Em. That sounds like a fun idea!" she said.

Mom crossed over into the living room and sat next to Dad.

"Dad and I loved how you two were getting along today, so we have an extra surprise. We're ordering pizza for dinner!"

Emmie dropped the bedding and pillows and did her happy dance. She shook it to the left and shook it to the right, wiggled her hands up and shimmied her shoulders. Pancake breakfast, ice cream lunch, pizza dinner, and a day spent with a unicorn! Aside from the fact that her sister could potentially be a unicorn forever, this was a pretty awesome day! From upstairs, the family heard a "Yay!" from Hannah, who had been listening in.

"Hannah will be down soon. I'm getting our fort ready!" Emmie said.

"Okay, you girls make your fort and set up your picnic area. When the pizza comes, I'll bring it down," Mom said.

"Thanks, Mom!" Emmie said.

"Yeah, thanks, Mom!" Hannah yelled from upstairs.

Emmie ran down to the basement, and an invisible Hannah met her shortly after. Emmie used the couch as a base for the fort, then draped the blankets over it. While Hannah nudged the pillows with her long snout, arranging them perfectly for the picnic area, Emmie returned upstairs for more blankets.

Perfect timing. The pizza was delivered while Emmie was upstairs, keeping their parents out of the basement. Emmie grabbed the box and took it downstairs. She made one more trip to get the extra blankets then returned downstairs to finalize the fort.

While she was gone, Hannah had found string lights and pulled them over to the fort with her giant unicorn teeth.

Emmie's eyes lit up. It was the ultimate pizza party, and it was about to get better. Hannah asked Emmie to do something Emmie never thought Hannah would ask her to do.

"Will you grab my phone and play some music?" she asked.

Emmie almost fell onto the freshly assembled fort. Use Hannah's phone to pick out music? Emmie had never felt so honored! Hannah picked the music, of course, but Emmie got to play DJ for the night. Once the playlist was assembled, the two cozied into their beanbags, and Emmie served up the slices on each sister's plate. Emmie giggled as Hannah wedged a slice between her hooves and nibbled on a stretchy piece of cheese. Hannah laughed, too.

At the end of dinner, Hannah stretched out and asked Emmie to turn down the music. She explained that sunset was soon and since she was still a unicorn, it was time for the two to accept their fate.

"It's time for us to say our goodbyes," Hannah said.

Emmie looked at Hannah, confused for a moment. She had gotten so used to seeing her sister as a unicorn that she had forgotten that they had a deadline to change her back. It was as if Emmie was seeing through the unicorn shell to her sister. A tear rolled down her face and splashed on Hannah's front leg.

"You don't have to go!" she cried.

"How would we explain this to people?" Hannah said.

"We could dye your coat and say you're the family pony!" Emmie said.

"But what about my horn?" Hannah said.

Seeing that her sister was starting to feel sad, Hannah nudged Emmie with her large snout.

"We'll always have the memory of today. Even if it means I'll be a unicorn forever, today was fun."

Emmie shrugged. She took a long breath in and exhaled.

"C'mon! Flying? Or how about my horn blowing glitter, sprinkles, and bubbles?"

Emmie held back a giggle. It was right at her lips, but she didn't want to be happy. Not now. She would give up all the glitter-blowing unicorns in the world if it meant having her sister back. Still, Hannah was right, and when she thought about the day, she couldn't hold back her smile any longer.

"And finding you in an alley, with your ice latte drenched unicorn hair!" Emmie said with a laugh.

Hannah attempted to scowl but joined in the laugh.

"And the police horse chasing us!" Hannah said.

"Oh, and, and Mom's bubble wrap dance!" Emmie said.

"She looked like she was playing the floor is lava! Do you remember playing that game?" Hannah asked.

"I do! But I don't think anyone would do it quite like Mom did today!" Emmie said, through giggles.

The two burst into full laughter and rolled

on the ground, just as they had after watching Mom tiptoe around the bubble-wrapped rug.

It was a laugh that is special to sisters: one that sounds of mischief, feels like understanding, and loves unconditionally. It was the realization that the two were thinking the same thing at the same moment. It was the sound of one sister's voice echoing from the other. Friends laugh with one another, but sisters share their laughter.

When the two sisters calmed their giggles, Emmie lay with her head on Hannah's horse-like back, catching her breath. She rested her hands on her belly.

Emmie felt very strange. Her eyes stung from crying, but her ribs were sore from laughter. How could she feel so happy and so sad at the same time? Hannah lifted her head from the floor but did not look at Emmie.

"Thank you for everything you did for me today. Not everyone would do what you did," she said.

"Of course, Hannah. You're my big sister!"

Hannah smiled, then tipped her head toward Emmie, allowing the Unicorn Princess tiara to slide down her horn. She nudged the tiara onto Emmie's head.

Emmie wiped away a tear and smiled in return.

"I'll always be your big sister," Hannah said.

"You'll always be my first friend," Emmie replied.

Tears were streaming down Emmie's face, and water welled in Hannah's large, hazel eyes. Hannah lowered her head to her hooves and cried into the floor. Emmie buried her face in Hannah's shoulder, wetting Hannah's fur with her tears. The sisters cried in unison, as they had laughed in unison. Emmie squeezed her sister tightly and noticed that Hannah's fur felt different. She lifted her head and saw Hannah—Emmie's sister who once was a unicorn—sitting next to her. Hannah was still crying and unaware that the spell was broken.

"Hannah!" Emmie said.

"It's okay, Emmie. I'll be okay," Hannah said, trying to be brave.

"But, Hannah! You're Hannah again!"

Hannah lifted her head and opened her eyes. She looked at her human hands, shocked. Then, she ran her fingers through her hair, then touched her knees. Hannah felt around her scalp for a horn, which was no longer there. She laughed through her tears, deep from her belly.

"I'm Hannah again!" she said.

Emmie joined her in laughing, and the two human girls embraced in the longest hug they had ever shared. When they broke away, Hannah wiped a tear from Emmie's eyes.

"I'm going to miss hanging out with you so much. I had a lot of fun today," Emmie said.

"We will hang out more, Emmie, I promise. But maybe instead of flying on a unicorn, we can try something less dangerous... like mini golf."

"Deal," Emmie said.

She knew that, as long as they were together, it would be fun. Regardless of where they went from here, she was thrilled to have her sister back!

The basement door's handle jiggled. Instinctively, Emmie looked at Hannah, who gasped. This time, Hannah didn't disappear. The girls exchanged glances and giggled.

"What are you two giggling about?" Mom said, giggling too.

"Just sister secrets!" Emmie said.

"Hannah, it seems like I haven't seen you all day!" Dad said. "How are you feeling?"

"Great! Turns out laughter was the best medicine."

Emmie and Hannah exchanged another knowing glance. They made room for their parents in their blanket fort, and Mom and

Dad joined. Dad put on a movie, and the four of them laughed and sang along. Before the evening ended, Dad suggested more family time the next day.

"What if we play horseshoes in the park?" he said.

Hannah and Emmie looked at each other with large eyes, then shook their heads.

"Never again!" Emmie said.

"We were thinking mini golf," Hannah said.

"And bubble tea," Emmie added.

For the rest of their lives, they would grow apart, only to grow together again. Friends would come and go, but Hannah and Emmie had a bond that would outlast everything. It was more than their great unicorn adventure. Emmie and Hannah were one another's first and forever friend.

ABOUT THE AUTHOR

Jodi Boyer spent her childhood under trees, dreaming of magical creatures and faraway lands. She is thrilled to share her debut novel, *Emmie and the Accidental Unicorn*, inspired by her nieces and brought to life by her own sisterly bond. Mrs. Boyer lives in Austin, TX, with her husband and their dog.

ABOUT THE ILLUSTRATOR

Rusty Boyer is a content writer and debut illustrator, hailing from Austin, TX. As a lifelong artist, Mr. Boyer spends his free time creating music and writing.

CPSIA information can be obtained
at www.ICGtesting.com
Printed in the USA
LVHW051230251120
672557LV00006B/979